Jonah
and the
Whale

Cover illustration by
Randy Hamblin

Story adaptation by
Sarah Toast

Interior illustrations by
Gary Torrisi

Interior art consultation by
David M. Howard, Jr., Ph.D.

Louis Weber, C.E.O.
Publications International, Ltd.
7373 North Cicero Avenue
Lincolnwood, Illinois 60646

ISBN: 0-7853-2220-5

PUBLICATIONS INTERNATIONAL, LTD.
• Rainbow is a trademark of Publications International, Ltd.

A long time ago, the Assyrian people, who lived in the city of Nineveh, were cruel and wicked. And God was very unhappy with them.

One day God spoke to Jonah, telling him to go at once to Nineveh and warn the people that God was going to punish them if they did not change their ways.

Jonah did not want to do what God asked because he was Hebrew, and the Assyrians were the Hebrews' enemies. He did not want to make the journey to warn such people.

Jonah wanted to get away from the Lord. He decided to go far away in the other direction from Nineveh.

Jonah packed some food and water in bags that he could carry. Then he set out on a journey for the seaside town of Joppa to find a ship that was headed for Tarshish. Tarshish was the farthest place that a person could sail to across the Great Sea.

When Jonah finally reached Joppa and found a ship bound for Tarshish, he paid his fare and went on board.

Jonah was very tired. He went down into the hold of the ship to sleep.

The ship set sail under clear blue skies. Once the ship was on the open sea, God hurled a great wind. Such a mighty storm blew up that the ship was in great danger of breaking apart on the huge waves.

The frightened sailors all threw the ship's cargo into the sea to make the ship lighter. Each sailor cried to his god to save them, but nothing helped. The storm continued to rage.

The ship's captain found Jonah and woke him up. He told Jonah to pray to his god, too, in hopes that Jonah's god might save them all.

The sailors asked Jonah where he came from. They asked him why this storm had come up to destroy them.

Jonah answered that he was a Hebrew who worshiped the Lord who had made the sea and the land. He told them he was running away from God and that was why God had made the mighty storm.

Then the sailors were even more afraid. They asked Jonah, "What is this that you have done?"

Jonah told the sailors, "Pick me up and throw me into the sea. Then the sea will quiet down for you, for I know that it is because of me that this terrible storm has happened."

The good sailors tried instead to row the ship back to land. But the sea grew more and more stormy. In desperation, the sailors finally picked up Jonah and threw him into the churning sea.

The waters grew calm at once. The sailors were amazed by God's power. They promised to worship God always.

Meanwhile, Jonah was about to drown. God then sent a huge whale to swallow him. Jonah was in the whale's belly for three days and nights.

Jonah prayed to the Lord from the belly of the whale. He thanked God for saving him from the storm and the sea and for keeping him alive in the whale's belly. God heard, and made the whale cough Jonah out onto the shore.

Once again God told Jonah to travel to Nineveh. This time, Jonah obeyed.

When Jonah arrived at Nineveh, he cried out, "In forty days, God will destroy Nineveh because of your wickedness!"

The people of Nineveh believed him and were sorry. To show that they had turned from sin, they wore rough clothes.

Even the king of Nineveh took off his rich robes. He decreed that no person should eat or drink. The king hoped that God would change His mind if He saw that the people had changed.

God forgave the people of Nineveh. This made Jonah angry.

Jonah complained about being sent so far to warn wicked people. He thought the enemy of the Hebrews deserved to be punished. He did not want God to forgive the people of Nineveh.

Then Jonah went outside Nineveh and sat down in the sun to wait and see what would happen to the city.

God made a bush grow quickly to give Jonah shade in the hot sun. Jonah was very grateful for the shade.

The next morning, God sent a worm to kill the bush. Then God caused a warm east wind and a hot sun.

Without the bush's shade to protect him from the sun, Jonah felt so ill that he said angrily to God, "It is better for me to die than to live."

Then God said to Jonah, "You did not grow the bush or even try to take care of it, and it lived only one day. Yet you are angry that it is dead. At the same time, you would have me destroy the city of Nineveh."

God said to Jonah, "I spared the people of Nineveh because I have cared for them for many years."

Jonah finally understood that God loves and forgives all who turn from sin and walk in His path, no matter who they are or where they come from.